Sprawled Asleep

David P. Miller

Nixes Mate Books
Allston, Massachusetts

Copyright © 2020 David P. Miller

Book design by d'Entremont
Cover photograph by Jane Wiley

All rights reserved. This book or any portion thereof may not be reproduced or used in any manner whatsoever without the express written permission of the publisher except for the use of brief quotations in a book review or scholarly journal.

ISBN 978-1-949279-21-4

Nixes Mate Books
POBox 1179
Allston, MA 02134
nixesmate.pub/books

For my father, Melton M. Miller Jr.
(November 15, 1933 – May 28, 2018)

"When will we lose the habit of explaining everything?"
– Francis Picabia (translated by Martin Marks)

Contents

I. More or Less Right Here

Third Story Roof Sitting	1
At Ten Degrees	3
Leaflet on Walking	5
Girl and Grackle	7
Our Grotto	9
Look at the Sky	10
Rest Stop, Tampa Bay	12
Stony Brook, Granite	14
Blue Fingertips	16
Gaze, or Don't	17
Absolutely No Idea	19
Triple-Arch Bridge	21
Trailing Her Die	23

II. The Trees and I Have Woken Up

You're It	26
Chance	27
Please Explain	28
Ten at Night	30
December Opens	32
Almost Not Foreign	33
Awake in the Sleeping Car	34

Landscape With Hilton	35
None of My Business	37
Kneeling Woman and Dog	40
Someone Else's Daughter	41
Translucent Man	43
Claustrophilia	44
The Small Hours of May	45

III. Phonemes and Silences

One Picture	47
See Your Hearing	48
Discarded School Instrument	49
Ruined Piano	50
Circa	53
In Lieu of a Plane Crash	56
An Eventual Introduction	58
December 8 1980	60
Another Poem about Fireflies	62
Friendly Ghosts	64
The Huffington Post or Whatever	66
It's a Grand Night For Singing	68
Half the Day is Night	70

Sprawled Asleep

I. More or Less Right Here

Third Story Roof Sitting

It's so geometrical up here.
Our house is flat-topped.
The other summits in view
make a child's drawing of peaks.
Wedge tops and gable triangles
asphalt-shingled in shades of charcoal,
brick oven browns, forest greens
scarred from exposure. Up above here
a panorama of three-sided tubes.
Seven brick chimneys, sisters
of one hundred twenty-five years,
sit their squareness as sentinels.

Sparrows speed by and lodge
on a twig at my head height.
Watch them breezing out on that limb.
The landscape is pleasure sidekicked with fear.
Vertigo calls from the sudden edge.
Without railings, this viewpoint
is bordered by neckbreak.
We've watched fireworks, shoveled snowdrifts
paltry feet from the vacant air.

The summer afternoon is empty.
One dormer window, venetian blind
drawn. Over the turquoise bodega,
another's tar beach with pergola,
fence, lawn furniture, nobody out.
Sounds of motor growl, tire chafe,
imperative honks. I'm alone,
rubber roof-spread warming my jeans,
with cloud-clustered green,
the maple seed pendants,
and this solo seagull, suspended.

At Ten Degrees

At ten degrees, most men of twenty-five
have finally abandoned short pants, although

the polar bear fellows persist
with their ice baptisms, for the brief titillation

of voyeurs like me, wrapping my face
in Velcro mask at the donut shop, while two

little brothers stare, one after the other,
wondering if there's a robbery in progress.

Skin blanketed but for eye ring patches,
I untuck my nose from my scarf to look

at branches grazing the Neponset River,
each twig-end cluster bearing discs like water-level

chandeliers. At this moment, a hawk
breakfasts on a pigeon, crimson stains

across snowpack outside the kitchen window,
watched by my wife as she bites an English muffin.

The snow groans underfoot, a complaint with each tread.
I pause in the walk, sparrows fall to the ground

like leaves scudding across the crusted surface.
I don't care to be sewn into long underwear all winter

though Mayflower ancestors endured it. But bone chill,
pine branches' agitation like a hive's dancing stasis,

beast roars of snowplows clearing parking lots,
this all undrowns Pacific islands – yes? I clutch the question

as I twitch the thermostat, hold the space heater close.

Leaflet on Walking

Why Walk?
Child's slalom around stodgy grownup legs after church.
Granite blocks afford chance foot massage.
November leaf-muck sets inline rollers beneath the soles.

Is Walking for Me?
Five inches of erupted streetcar tracks.
Blue pen caricatures on Styrofoam shards wedged into chain-link.
Swallowed coastline incised in paving stone.

How Do I Get Started?
Hands off the sofa's velour arm: two steps pell-mell facedown to the carpet.
A stranger's elbow at the curb as the bus sighs open.
That swarm behind the breastbone at the doorsill: the old complaint.

What About Side Effects?
Five miles of heartbreak pounded through the ankles.
Downpour-drenched clothes worn to the smokehouse.
Four hands become three as two ramble the riverbank.

Are There Support Groups in My Area?
Downtown gaggles baffle the orange Wait hand.
Thin sidle past double baby carriage as suitcases roll through the portal.
Eyes met, downcast, eyes shifted, eyes bore straight ahead.

To Learn More
Graffiti-plastered brick factory vanished from the map.
Opaque quartz massaged by Sound waters.
Former opossum crumbled at the stone bridge.

Girl and Grackle

These embankment stones once hefted locomotives
above brewery workers' ceilings.
The eighteen-nineties shouldered trains
against a comb's-teeth set of dead-end streets.
Doll factory, pool hall,
lunch rooms, violin maker's shop,
now erased into a greenbelt park.
The stones at rest, lowered to our level,
skirt the playgrounds, hold rainwater
in pockmarks shaped like cumulus.

With last night's rain, a stone reflects
two pines' fringes bent to center.
A girl just tall enough to peek
into the water mirror
puts her finger there and wiggles
for the wetness on her skin. The trees
disappear in surface burbles.
Her mother and the stroller
gone toward the green, she spurts to catch up.
She's only now almost too big a girl
to wedge herself into the stroller seat.

The August puddle settles.
The pocket cavity outlines a thunderhead
in granite. The pines again
reach for each other, submerged
beneath narrow slips of yellow
locust leaves, pale needles'
random webwork.
A grackle stops, bends for a sip,
and the treetops vanish.

Our Grotto

I remember you as a telephone voice, pealing your name.
Female artist guised as a bat that fifth of July,
re-guised as a woman now sighing
                                  in midwinter bathtub.
With gold-plated grapefruit spoons, windowed bonsai.

Wings of Desire and the miles' walk to your room.
Split grapefruit sugared and squeezed late that July,
then flat-mate's stiff outrage: odd man in the bathroom.
Now cities of bookshelves, childhood piano,
                                        pine tree bonsai.

As a woman you surfaced in newsprint,
                                        withheld your name.
Female artist sugared my pen, eared like a bat
homed toward new eaves, your bedroom our grotto.
Skittered across arsoned lots for the same

two knocks at your window, over the gnome
                                      in his dome below stairs.
I remember your fire demon, futon overseer
                                          in paint that July.
The eureka girlfriend, my only she: even midwinter
is honeyed with greening like our bonsai.

Look at the Sky

Pinned and plunging beneath the flat
of a thunderhead, a thick purple-
bruised ceiling more threatening
than night's translucent black.
The bus scrambled out
from beneath that dark table,
toward the blue shelf
opened at the horizon.

I can write *thunderhead*. Or write
these: *horsetails, lenticular,
buttermilk sky*. What I want:
to exhale *ah! altostratocumulus*.
To know the mundane sky
direct as knowing the breath.
No study or action of mind.

Cloud guides, books for unveiling weather.
I have read them. They don't take.
For the figure of this very instant,
I fumble back to the picture book index.
What up above are those again?
My want may as well be a koan
assigned by a roshi of atmosphere.

I can write *misty blue dusk,*
black ragged puffs
in a cluster. They passed
over the window glass.
Then they dissolved out of my sight.
Or coagulated, I don't know which.
I feel breeze through the screen.
It has dropped, and with it the curtain.

Rest Stop, Tampa Bay

De Soto made landfall more or less right here
where the tourists let loose the dogs
along this curtailed patch of beach,
south of the Sunshine Skyway Bridge.

A desolate, abandoned village met
De Soto when he made landfall here.
We find a fist-sized conglomerate rock
along this curtailed patch of beach.

Striated imprints of twenty thumbnail shells,
abandoned homes of desiccated scallops, met
by mud and eons' complacent pressure.
A fist-sized conglomerate rock

with trilobite's mud-brown ghost pressed underside.
Striated imprints of twenty thumbnail shells:
limestone chalk highlights the banded arcs.
Out of mud and eons' complacent pressure

this grey stone matter appears to eye and hand.
With mud-brown trilobite pressed to the palm
it cups securely in my grasp.
Limestone chalk brightens banded arcs,

hairs'-width brushstrokes across a blunted wedge.
Grey stone matter appears to eye and hand
a tool to strike, a fragment to split.
It cups securely in the grasp,

thumb, index, middle fingers clasp
shell impressions edging this blunted wedge.
I think this had been chiseled out, hewn as
a tool to strike, a rock fragment to split

oysters. Along this curtailed patch of beach
thumb, index, middle fingers clasp
a fantasized prehistoric souvenir. I want to
think this had been chiseled out, hewn

and left behind long before De Soto, dropped
among the oyster shells. This patch of beach
features a dog named Charlie, snuffling toward us
and our wishful prehistoric souvenir.

South of the Sunshine Skyway Bridge,
a patch of beach where the dogs let loose,
a village found abandoned at De Soto's landfall,
more or less right here.

Stony Brook, Granite

Stony Brook shears the corner of Martin's
Barber Shop, makes five sides of a rectangle.
Tunneled under the path rising to the park,
Stony Brook repudiates buildings' weight.

Pass the barber and a patch of nine corn plants,
three staked tomatoes. *Cultivado
por voluntarios*, says the stubbed wood stake.
The path paved over water lifts to the green.

Alternate-leaf dogwood throws a runner
of cream petals over pavement. Pines,
then oaks, fall away toward quick-built
mansard homes for brewery workers. Stony Brook
was fed on brewer's waste. Fouled and buried.

At the basketball court, taut-bodied parents
teach their sons skateboarding. Mom
with blue wings inked about her shoulder blades,
water and snacks in a Trader Joe's bag. Dad
in rainbow reggae t-shirt and camo shorts.
Two shaghead boys practice not falling off.

Rough granite blocks scored with rips and drill holes
edge the ball court, pocket gardens, paved meanders.
Lifted down from an embankment that raised a railbed,
down to comfort the park with stone.

At the green's far end, five raise yogic torsos
from the earth. They rise where the railbed isn't.
Across the street, the subway station names
the Brook, interred, flowing, and forgotten.

Blue Fingertips

Out of the flood of high-schoolers
who saturate this bus wall to wall,
a long tall young woman,
her hair gathered high overhead,
plugs the gap next to me.
She whips fast through
Chinese flash cards done by hand,
jabs the characters with her finger,
moves her lips with each, flip flip
flip. Crams the deck inside
a lime-green box, stuffs the
box in her backpack, rifles the pack
for a book. Grabs her pen.
It's broken. She stares shocked
at her wet blue fingertips,
motions them about
like new and strange things.
The old guy at her side, me,
hands her a wad of tissues.
An olive-shaded woman across the aisle
hands her a spare pen. The girl thanks us,
begins furiously underlining
her paperback of *Brave New World*.

Gaze, or Don't

He is not likely dead. Men never die
on the subway with legs
casually crossed at the knees.

Men with white ponytails
spiked behind pattern-bald
tonsures don't kick the bucket
in loose-looped cravats
of red and black paisley.

Men in shirts of Egyptian cotton,
suede shoes of charcoal grey,
slumped at the railings in end seats,
chins at their chests, wide woven hats
upside down at their feet,
are: asleep.
     Asleep at the end
of the line and asleep
when the train switches back.
Sleeping for us who gaze, or don't,
at scaly red arms, the flushed crown
of a head, smart slim-fit jeans.

See, his fingers are twitching.

Everyone leaves him alone. Him and
his hat. Nobody steps on his hat.
Nobody hands him his hat.
Nobody asks him his stop.
An elderly elegant gent,
shuttling through the rush hour,
who is not dead.

Absolutely No Idea

Sorry she grins to the young beard at her right
after twice rolling toward him. *Sorry.*
The beard smiles, doesn't mind
her low sleeveless diaphanous whatever.
Sorry to the dude with earbuds at her left
after half leaning over his lap. Man Two
scowls toward the off-campus short-shorts:
You keep saying Sorry.

Her voice at her friend on the phone
flows toward tears. Doesn't break
though. One, two subway stops, three.
She half leans up each time, asks
    Where is this?
Standee woman in front of her
rides the car floor as if it were
Tuesday Not Party Night. Which it is.
Asks what Sorry girl wants, where she's
going. What exactly she's doing.

Harvard Square she wants.
The wrong line. Wrong
direction. Wrong,
all of it.

Out, across the next station platform,
having processed more than one
verbal instruction. We hope.
She, unrooted, too easily stripped
by the eye. I want

her parents. The back seat
of their car. Her, sprawled asleep
in a drive home past her bedtime
after ice cream.

Triple-Arch Bridge

Frank Bolles passed here in sunrise
on a walk to the Blue Hill, winter eighteen-ninety.
He recorded *the pretty triple-arch bridge
over the Neponset*. Snow fleas
beguiled him, though the view was *injured
by the smoke of Boston* from cellars of coal.

I've plodded that Quincy granite span
twenty-five years. Paul's Bridge.
I fancied it a saunter, seated half-lotus
with neighborhood muffin and coffee,
twenty minutes of riverbank watch
before hauled back on my feet,
up-street to the college. Puzzling
Paul who? Who Paul?

Then Dunkin' Donuts squatted a derelict
gas station, knocked out the local
donut and lunch place. Nothing
museful about toting Dunkie's
Neponset-side: I gave it up.
Pneumonia culled Bolles at thirty-eight.
I tramp across Paul's at sixty, a glance
at the water for heron or ducks.

Didn't used to see wild turkeys
in those river-watch years,
ganged, possed, or raftered
as they are now, across the lawns
up Brush Hill Road. The birds refrain
from attacking this foot commuter,
so far. Though a hurtling deer
nearly bowled me over.

For Bolles, snow fleas. Now turkeys
and deer spill from Blue Hill
to here. Sixty-four deer
taken out in a December cull.
"I was the lucky first one"
said the first man to topple a legal doe
since Frank Bolles ended his
thigh-deep tramping through
Land of the Lingering Snow.

Trailing Her Die

Tower Street, thirty degrees sharp.
Climb to Forest Hills Cemetery's
side iron gate. Diagonal neighborhood:
funeral parlor roots the ascent's first steps.
A German Shepherd watches me, wary,
as her master phones in a ruptured pipe.
A home with two wooden emblems:
butterflies underscore *Welcome*,
sunburst adorns *No Trespassing*.
At the top, the street opens to pines,
unnamed puddingstone monuments.

Into the files of slabs and inscriptions,
I'm trailing her die. She an eminent
permanent resident, my map marks the route
to her family stone and all the way back.

No one is here. Scuff the new snow, track toward
Summit Avenue. The silence of near-arrival
replaced by traffic's hiss. Winter's first fall:
slide and topple. I curse and mutter myself
to my feet, look for a tomb topped with detritus.
Her name surmounted with acorns, twigs.

Pheasant feather. Metal cufflink. Two red pebbles
with white paint mottoes: *Communication*
says one, the other effaced but for — r — .
Brown roses wrapped in cracked plastic
next to her footstone.

Return to the gate, past the chapel where I heard
a poet eff her out loud, her suicide,
the horse she rode in on. Two more inattentive
collapses. Descending, the Shepherd now placid,
her master holds palaver with a deliveryman.
At the busway, a step into Spanish *palabras*.
A girl carries a fragile collage,
six blue feathers and tissue,
across puddles and aboard to her seat.

For Anne Sexton

II. The Trees and I Have Woken Up

You're It

Has it come yet? the Dean of Men stage-
whispered, as the boyish engineer
stepped ahead, reached out for his diploma.
His strident *sotto voce* cut across
the university commencement. *It* was me.
The zoology professor's daughter
sped to the hospital to labor while my father
nabbed his bachelor's.
                        We all were *its*
before we crossed the water, made the gate.
Who knew its likely sex (one or maybe more),
its being hale or failing, living or called back?
David or Sara.

But I hit the snooze alarm. Refused my entrance,
pouted in the dressing room another seven days.
Gave the lie to *Stork Beats Sheepskin*,
the trigger-happy human interest headline.
One week till I agreed
to one more of ten thousand encores,
opened my eyes to everything that was the case,
still is the case. Began again and wailed.

Chance

Nothing other than a fading chance,
but chance favors the prepared mind,
as Louis Pasteur thought. Maybe it was luck
that what she wrote is what I read –
avowed heterosexual, she said,
seeks an auspicious coincidence.
Half-inch of newsprint and my scanning sight.
It was either luck or long-gestating chance
that meant I found her writings twice.
After two replies she let me hear her voice.

I had worked hard to make my luck:
overworked, it crumbled like desiccated clay.
Came to renounce expectation –
but read the paper anyway.
And found what Pasteur may have known:
chance also favors the prepared heart,
empty of tactics, certainty, and hope.

Please Explain

At twelve I found new vinyl at the library.
Vernal-bloomed electronic riot, floodtide
feedback hum, table-saws of broken wire.
Underrumbles rose to square-wave throats.
Tin plate rivets swept the speaker space,
fell to tiny aftercycles. Baffled, indulgent
Mother peered from kitchen work, asked me:
"David, do you *understand* this?"

Intermission in the men's room. Two gents
inform each other, as well as every denizen
of stall and urinal, of connoisseur's critique
affixed already to this fledgling play.
goddamn it keep your cerebrating
virus to yourselves: I'd slam my palms
over my ears were hands available to slam.

I've overheard *the point* demanded of a roughened
slate grey canvas crossed with black house-
painter brushstrokes. Or one entirely in eggshell.
Or unprimed, marked with spasmodic scribbles,
a lost orthography's automatic writing.
The point: concept without dimension, purely

theoretical. See now, even to be
seduced by *point* renders language bloodless.

Amber floor lamplight cast on a warped
window shade. Call the shape a duck.
Fifty thousandth rounding of the air, hollowed
in an open trench. Call the sound a subway.

I listen to the old LP again. Amplified continents
slide apart, brush aurora drone layers.
Hammered circuit jabs, scrabbling wire scrapes.
I still don't understand. The duplicate creature
who shares my breath and synapses, blood vessels,
optic nerves and tympani, leaves marks behind
on paper. But cannot deduce this, disembodied.
Plunges toward the thing and rises, plunges and rises.

Ten at Night

Young ailanthus leaves flutter their fingertips
in orange streetlight. My eardrum clicks.
Headlights pass without comment.

A woman ambles her bulky dog
along the sidewalk. Their bodies
retreat in the streetlight's aura
like decaying Polaroids.

Streetlight sifted
through the maple back yard
mottles the next door house:
orange algae fluorescent
on a black pond.

Curtainless window two yards behind,
light plotted across the ceiling. Curios range
the sill. An elbow flicks across
the glass. Then a whole human torso
in blue sweater, caramel hair, bends,
stretches an arm to blackout.

Auto toots burp against
the refrigerator's long mutter.
New rain scat-bangs the metal gutter
as I arch from the futon
to shut the light.

December Opens

The window glass is old and ripples light.
The trampoline next door is still.
A spray of branches rooted out of sight

wavers just above the sill.
A spate of morning sparrows leaps to eat
while squirrels glean bird-feeder spill.

Ailanthus leaves lie guttered in the street
as shadows slip from siding, down
to vanish at the margin where yards meet.

December opens mild and brown.
Neighbor fences waver through the glass.
Outside the window, bamboo sounds

its winter clack, suspended in a mass
of brittle voices, chimed and bright.

Almost Not Foreign

Picture no escape from her nursing home
television, booted each waking. At twilight
no way to sequester near
a hushed window's beauties,

bathed in cricket calls' lapsing time. Babel
forever foreign: invading hallway light, worrying
attendants, chasm in front of soup. Imperceptible

her drift from unwilling guest, braced to
bust out of here, to ghost: fallen to silence,

unable to perceive her husband, asking
Daddy? – this man almost not foreign
as muscles petrify, words lapse.

Command her wedding pictures, beauties
of the hour at nineteen. Sequester
the final, frightened twilight. Afterlife
or none, stand back for her escape.

Awake in the Sleeping Car

The orange rabbit-faced moon
skews its eyes down sideways,
just above the shadowed horizon
behind snowfields blacked out
at dusk. Our lingering, languid
train leaves Schenectady.
The moon's avatar rises
in neon over brick:
script-entwined G and E
in a great green radiant circle.
The spheres attend
this little population on rails
passing in the new-fallen night,
lagging late hours toward home.

Landscape With Hilton

Help a lady out? Skin-stretched,
skeletal, she holds a paper cup

amid a wash of playgoers leaving
hip-hop opera as they drop toward Market.

A waitress brings grilled cheese and slaw
in a faux-Fifties diner next street downhill,

emaciated and bald beneath
a jaunty blue kerchief, metal-red-lipped,

uneasily young and worn over the bones.
Past top-hatted doormen in capes

that swallow the light, taxi-whistling,
someone with square-trimmed beard,

pierced crystal eyes, neither starved
nor naked, stalks shouting

against his best mind.
Slide one block to the Tenderloin –

pale block letters against brick
remember *Elegantly Furnished Rooms*

*Private Phones Steam Heat
Hot Water Elevator Service*

Private Baths $20 Month.
Above the sidewalk, a voided sign

for a vanished café, shaft rising
toward Corinthian columns and satellite dish,

overpainted entirely in white.

None of My Business

I'm sitting right behind the plate glass
of this locavore store-café. They don't
ever look back, the people inches away
outside.   Case in point: a guy with black
studded wrist bands, black cutoffs, stud-
ded black zipped bag hung at the waist.
Some kind of hunk of rough cloth
drapes his torso, fastened
at the middle but open
to a side view of pecs, inviting
pec peekers which I'm normally not
but now sort of am temporarily,
ugh. It's because of his tattoo, though:
"2 + 2 = [cat silhouette]".
Also because of his woman friend
in a black one-piece with
Stedelijk Museum Amsterdam
shoulder bag. See, I've been there
so I know something she knows.
This doesn't make me cool
like her, but makes me cooler
than I would look if they looked
at me sitting at this counter.

Next: boy and girl, let's say,
it's what they'd probably call themselves.
Across the street, her back
against the giant butterfly-faced
Mexican mask mural. Presses her palms
between her legs while she
looks up at the boy through
sunglasses. Removes her shades,
relaxes her thighs. Now
observation is chancy because
people not right at my window
are more inclined to look back.
That may be a nervous glance
my way, from her.
This old man.

It's ninety-five degrees.
Beneath his t-shirt, a fellow hauls
something resembling county-fair,
all-time record-setting,
prize-winning produce. I imagine
a proud little girl posing
for the rural newspaper with
her astounding squash or watermelon.
Still, all things in balance,

his backpack is miniature, lime green.
Sir, nobody wants you to collapse
in the intersection as you lurch, looks like,
through this heat index horror tale.

Kneeling Woman and Dog

Six pm at a window seat. Looking at the dark
through snowflake cutouts and lettering backwards.
Over the lip of an evening's red-eye,
I watch a woman kneel on the sidewalk.
She strokes a small dog tied to a post.
Caresses the dog in silence.
The black dog receives her caresses.
Kneeling woman and her dog, I think,
in a glacier wind.

She rises and turns away from the dog.
She'll come back, she assures it, I think.
Minutes lapse, the polar air nips its fur.
A man approaches and the dog jumps wagging.
Man unties dog: they leave the post.

So it wasn't her dog in that polar air.
Or else for five minutes
it was her dog. She belonged to it too,
finding it tethered and alone.

Someone Else's Daughter

The train pulls right, it was at rest, now it moves,
or now as it moves it hurries, gains trackage
per moment. Your torso ticks left.
You put yourself upright. You can do this
with your eyes closed. Or the other way:
it slows to cover less ground per inbreath,
per outbreath. So your torso ticks right
on the metallic cloth seat. You right yourself
again and your head points to noon.
It's half past five and your eyes were open
all day. The car was yours alone when
you sat down, let your lids fall.

The same train on the same rail
enters the same tunnel. Two faithful
train-on-track tones: the upper
thickens as tunnel walls resound
overtones against the body. Remember
how your dog always sat up when the Rambler
slowed, two turns before the house?
The train returns to open air and you rise,
open eyes, the dog coming home.

Two sandals on the floor with feet in them.
Skinny legs in cutoffs. The torso and arms
of a teenage girl. So now two people
in the car. Her face, cheeks glazed
with salt water. Her soundless shudders.
She pulls her eyebrows together
at the folded tissues from your pocket,
offered to someone else's daughter.

It's OK, they're clean.
                                        Thank you.

The same arriving bell. The same
open-door thunk. The same car
with a new solitary occupant.

Translucent Man

A man hunches over a slab counter, hummus sandwich,
café stool facing a window wall. Blue-black outside.

His dark double-visioned outline in the glass.
Walkers abandon cubicles, shuffle to parking garage,

tear through his reflected membrane. Nylon jacket
falls toward a hung chest cavity, portal to night.

Bowed forehead rests against a taillight's
red caution. One hand flexes, translucent fingers

stroke a delivery truck. Walkers bob
under mirrored hanging cone-lamps:

unaware party-goers in phantom lampshade hats.
Taxi-top skims his scalp, pauses for a traffic cop:

Make College More Entertaining: the message
blazoned above his winter rush hour cranium.

Claustrophilia

You take my hand beneath the covers,
lace my fingers among yours.
Sweetheart, the phalanx bones sigh.

The Small Hours of May

The trees and I have woken up
before dawn. Perhaps they were
already aroused. There was breeze
rustling their chlorophyll palms,
sometime back in the blackness
before the night's final train
murmured two blocks from our windows.
Well, if the trees suffered insomnia
while I was bound in a labyrinth dream,
we're all awake now. It's moonless,
sunless, and what bird is this
so rhapsodic in the dark?
It's a question not to answer
lying still in a bedsheet,
eyelids prone, mind all in my ears
with the notes of this singer
who graces one of the listening,
drowsy, trees.

III. Phonemes and Silences

One Picture

And when I thought the poem was done,
two dozen birds rose from the trees,
sank back. And when I thought, again,
the poem was done, five cows
appeared in silhouette,
ambled out of frame.

See Your Hearing

Listener, burnish the sense
where it is felt, each jewel, sound-being.
Air's voices shift as skull pivots,
left side and right, six directions
set in unwavering mind.

My scatterhead's listening checklists
church chimes' humid auroras,
mosaic clatter from startled bird babies,
flat thump of cardboard on plastic.
Heard that. Heard this. The roster ticked.

Packed earbuds guard concentration's thin gate.
Play it again: repeat, fade, decay.
Repetition fabricates foreplay for the ears,
but with bare attention stillness' pulse shines.

Now you, see your hearing. Introspect
sound in your skull's heaven: lustrous percepts.
Each beat, rasp, slide, crack, sigh,
manifest like honey, like water, like night.

Discarded School Instrument

You were never a real violin to me.
That made us an ideal match. I could never
have been your musician. You, uncovered
in a friend's basement in my weak flashback.
You with three flaccid strings, tuning
pegs slack in their holes. A bow dried
beyond hope of rosin. What can a hurt instrument
do, being still a thing with its body?
We scraped a drone against Reagan, president
with three six-letter names, six six and six.
Rome roasted, so I sawed across your carcass.

Now I find you prone in the attic, memory
of a memory, corpse of a corpse, still
in your case withering to cardboard.
This is the day to remove you, unlock
the patch of bare floor you squat.
Replace you with no other old saved thing.
The attic was all forgetfulness, but
its great emptying-out begins with you.

Ruined Piano

after the music of Ross Bolletter

Goggled men in orange jackets
take sledgehammers to a bootless piano,
a swayback banished to pasture.
The only sounds the creature utters
the crackings of wood flown to fragments,
whack of soundboard fallen to
concrete. Or sent end over end
down two flights to the parking lot,
carapace popped
as a turtle meets a mean boy
with a ball peen.
These are smashed pianos.
These are not ruined pianos.

Set a fire inside an old upright.
Place it upon a stone plaza at dusk.
A fireplace of wood,
falling to char. Tongueless,
strings melted, its only sound
the roiling of flames against air.
This is an auto-da-fé'd piano.
It is not a ruined piano.

A ruined piano was pushed to the all-weather porch
and forgotten, or escorted out to the barn.
A ruined piano wandered outdoors
and nobody called it back home.
Immigrant ruined pianos were left on the shore.
A ruined piano waits in the rehearsal room
as accompanists stroke the younger piano.

A ruined piano won't speak as it should.
Stuck zipper voice. It smiles
and a drawerful of forks falls to the floor.
Table-sawn syllables. Step dance
in a suitcase of mud. Chime clusters
tuned to its brainwaves. Notes fricate
back of its teeth. Coughs collapse
into its body, ricochet metal spit.

Aluminum ice storms. Tobacco-wrecked gabble.
Temple bells made of old pans. Horseshoe nails
against slate. Warehouse of domino-fallen
doorframes. Dump truck emptying granite.

Heartbeat of ball bearings. Clacked bones
in the throat.

A ruined piano, wedding gift
for a perfect pitch mother. A ruined piano
cuddles field mice. A ruined piano
somehow came with the house.
A ruined piano is at least
out of the way.

Circa

"4 + 20," this song I've always nearly forgotten from
the album where Stills Crosby Nash
                                      set up with Young. Against
an almost vacant Saturday brunch room, except
for me and a sometimes applauding handful,
                                        he sings it between
"Blackbird" (verses scrambled) and
                         "Dead Oligarchs" which, despite
its hopeful title, is his wordless acoustic
                                      to end the set. He's circa

my own age, it gets harder to tell, songbook circa
my time as adolescent watcher-
                                        of-The-Revolution from
the TV set in what we called the family room, despite
the fact that the family was in every room.
                                          Mouth up against
microphone, so tight it swallows
                                   all his consonants. Between
songs he's clear as an enunciating bell, except

for some throwaway jokes off mike
                                      that dribble faint. Except
for the 45 of "Hurdy Gurdy Man" I wore down,

                                                then lost circa
Reagan's re-election, his Donovan would
                        fail me now, between
vowel tones crooned too deeply
                        and zero treble response from
the eatery's sound rig. But teenage memory
                        catches against
his unintended mutter, and lyrics blossom
                        almost in despite.

Stephen Stills' song lifts me an aging smile, despite
the voice in the lyric
                        having driven his woman away. Except
for my knowing nothing
                        much about Stills to set against,
I'd always made this one an uneasy confessional,
                        me circa
ten years younger than twenty-four
                        when I slipped the disc from
its *Déja Vu* jacket, nestled alphabetically between

Let It Be and my only B.B. King. Stills' age lay between
my girlfriendless kidhood and my divorce. Despite
my skittish eye at "the many-colored beast" from
a death-worried last verse, no details in "4 + 20"
                        there was nothing to except
out of a lost love I hadn't yet found. It took circa

four of my years added to Stills'
      before there was that rubble to clash against.

In the Saturday brunch spot all is forgiven,
                              nothing against
the maladjusted P.A. My eggs and toast
                      in the middle between
my fellow relic behind his acoustic
                      and a Peter Wolf pic circa
2010. Wolf looking pretty damn
                      long in the tooth, despite
eye makeup and ever-rockin' grimace.
                  Head-shaking stuff, except
that these folks are best snugged
                  with the music they're from.

Stills' acoustic peals persist in head-music
                  between thoughts, except
when Donovan's drum breaks ripple my memory
                        despite them. Circa
childhood's edge, from then on
          this body is what rock breaks against.

In Lieu of a Plane Crash

no one's ever lost forever / when they die they go away / but they will visit you occasionally / do not be afraid – Amanda Palmer

Squatting O'Hare Gate K8
ravished by Amanda Palmer
inside my noise suppression oasis.
Listening I should not do in public.
Lachrymose men nearly sixty
should not be seen at K8 or any Gate.

There's a couple just like us
if we were hard-bit tough.
Smokes, burnt-in tans.
She leans back across the seat
cradles her head on his shoulder as
yours and mine on the subway sometimes.

Wrong Way Turn Back Now flight to
Vegas. Twenty-six hundred miles
against a blaring red light.
Two years ago I hurtled southwest
and your father died.
This is one reason I am scared.

Situation Room on a screen
hanging like Damocles' sword
can't message me out of this cattle drive.
The little Aussie geckomatronic
fails to charm. Glacier melt
as coming attraction:
the volume shocks up.

Now stuff ourselves like olives
inside a tube of reinhaled oxygen.
Wait to be gagged out
toward one hundred eight degrees
and newsboxes of *Little Naked Darlings*.

Count back from eighty-three hours
till I find your breath again in the dark.

An Eventual Introduction

As if carpeted by acne,
as if my voice caromed
from boy soprano to baritone,
I was the one who choked out
syllables of admiration during intermission.
      Oh, one of those thousands.
You were seventy, I forty years
behind. Bothered grandfather,
you nodded, a slight strain
toward interest. I fell back
unmanned, toward a phalanx
of friends who thought me expert
where you were concerned.

You were jumped by a punk
on Sixth Avenue. Sunk to the floor
a month after, brain's blood
cut off, at seventy-nine
more quiet
than your two hundred plants.

I waked you all night the next winter,
read your *Empty Words* aloud

for eight hours. Listeners
lingered, left. Dawn emerged
through fog. Your poem
dispersed to phonemes
       and silences.
Students with sleeping bags,
determined final hearers,
applauded the grey light.

for John Cage

December 8 1980

So what the hell am I supposed to do?
Just put a Band-Aid on it?
—John Lennon

Mister Lennon? calls the
lapsed Beatles believer, born again
as self-made Hound of Heaven.
Fourteen years after *bigger than Jesus*,
that top-of-the-pops blasphemy,
former fanboy puts four hollow-point bullets
through the artist's left side.

College mate Andy's voice falters
from the wall phone in my sloped-
floor apartment. Our man is disappeared,
his *watching the wheels* unspun.
His left eyeglass-lens hematic for the cameras.

Circumstance's ragged wheel
inert. Ticking without apparent intent.
A wheel unwatched until
it recoils, strikes random. Two through
the shoulder. Four-fifths blood sacrifice,
hypovolemic shock.

November. The pompadour of
good clean hate annihilates
the Georgia peanut farmer.
December. The *Enquirer* monetizes
Lennon's wax face in profile
on the slab. Adrift

at my quarter-century,
in the ramshackle dump
where the first marriage ends,
I say to Andy
nothing I now remember.

Another Poem about Fireflies

We say "listen to the wind in the trees"
but that is not the sound. What is the sound
of a leaf moving? How many leaves
in these after-dark silhouettes framed
by highway horizon glow? I came to the porch
because I heard a gentle rainfall
but it was not water mist against leaves.
It was leaves against the movement of air.
We cannot hear air, cannot hear one
two three leaves change position.
But this, sounding of indrawn breath
and tide drawn back across black
volcanic pebbles, this we can hear.

I came to the covered porch to be misted
this July dusk but there was not mist.
There were pulsing tree trunks. There were events
at the edges of my eyesight, and when I looked
they were bugs. Then there were more events
that when I looked again became lights.
I don't remember when I last saw
fireflies, and I don't know if I will ever
see them again. So stark, their white-yellow signals

pull from deep in the yard across the street,
and down the street. Each its own light-
point cycle, so many aerial lighthouses.
Flash cycle nebula densing the more
the more I abandon eye focus. This erratic
point cloud beneath tides of treetops,
and me in the fade to black, secure
in my simple irrelevance to all of it.

Friendly Ghosts

When alone at night,
it's best to keep your mouth shut.

You can pull down the old LP set,
hear Cyril Ritchard reading *Alice* as you sat
with your grandfather at five years.

You can find your Bowie albums,
dream yourself back to college,
ears thrust toward the stereo.

You can reread Beckett's *Not I*,
replay Billie Whitelaw's voice
as you listened paralyzed
before a video in the side gallery.

You can find yourself online,
listen to yourself read
one of your own poems,
if you can bear it.

You can hear your late mother's voice,
your late father-in-law's,
permanent residents
where brain meets mind.

When alone at night,
no need to move your lips.
You can abandon the chatter.
The friendly ghosts surround you.

The Huffington Post or Whatever

You could let your eyesight cling a long time
to the 1940s portrait of their engaged, beaming faces,
temples nuzzled for the studio photographer,
his Navy collar and her pearl earrings, their dreamland
smiles, and you will definitely back up back to it
after checking out the thing about this white
most beautiful girl in the world
who is only nine years old, but probably
not the celebrity next link over who went
from hot to heavy in kind of the same bikini
at least according to the photograph.

You could sink into the image of them
in their narrow beds pushed together,
dying at home five hours apart, holding hands
till the husband went, releasing the clasp
of his wife with dementia, and wonder what she knew
in that moment. And this is a sad thing to you as is
the whole idea of a three-year-old boy, frozen to death
locked outside in a diaper. I mean,
there are some people you will just never understand.
And it turns out the *Pimp My Ride* cars
were just totally faked-up after all.

You could make yourself realize that sixty-seven years
of marriage, through kidney failure and Alzheimer's,
smashes anyone's oldfangled cynicism, that sterile
world-weary stunt, and how *I can't live without you*
is a literal truth woven into ten braided fingers.
And that the five famous onscreen couples
who didn't like each other in real life
might have been happier if there were a way
to regrow lost hair. Though this might not have helped
the stay-at-home mom who spills it that
"my husband was my rapist."

Why don't you know why
Reese Witherspoon's black-and-white
Oscars dress looked so familiar?
Why did you miss this year's saddest
Oscars moment? Why don't you
pay more attention? You let it all slide
right by you, like how terrific Keira Knightley looked
pregnant at the Oscars. Two caskets at the funeral home.
Their daughter's tears. And do sweethearts have
our song any more like when he was in the service?
You'll ponder this again after a quick moment
for this other thing, shedding fifteen years'
mortgage payments with only one dirty little secret.

It's a Grand Night For Singing

It's the usual cramped hustle between platforms.
Blue tarps and green scaffolds narrow the passage
down and elbowed around the vague gapers
who possibly know where they're headed
but hesitate and rotate below my speed, well
anyway, I find little vacancies to slip between.

Left in my wake, a baritone warbler I almost don't hear.
People sing in the subway, but this is so odd, a voice
of deep mahogany. Not like the flattened
tune-shapes chanted by men (always men)
following their earbuds' commands.

Landed and ready, I bulldozed to no avail.
A ten minutes' wait. The croon approaches,
patient, nearing, a church choir cornerstone.
And I know what he sings – how? This
something that's maybe *more than the moon,
maybe it's more than the birds*

*maybe it's more than the sight of the night,
in a light too lovely for* words
I want to shut out because I'm ten again,

my mother has choral group ladies
around the piano, downstairs
after bed and I want quiet. Boy galaxy
of boy planet circling boy star,

it's all me, weary of hearing the starts
and stops of this same same music.
For my mother, her women,
it's all *a grand night for singing.*
Each time again, they insist,
the earth is a-glow
and to add to the show,

I think I am falling in love
he booms behind me, gray braid
poked from cloth cap, two-wheeled cart
with trash bag liner, umbrella handle
at the lip. He pushes toward the far end,
his own audience,
falling, falling in love.

Half the Day is Night

Crisp in the ears, and crisp beneath your shoes,
the chill shelters your skin, crackles around
your feet. The shock of color massed in canopies
is silence, muted mind, dilated sight.

The equinox at autumn is a hinge,
a pivot tacking August sog and scrape
to winter's pulse stripped to astringent breath.
Mind clarifies as summer's malice dies.

I sit outside this dark September night.
The hand of dusk across my heart, my spine
caressed by stillness. The listening to come
to what there is to hear when nothing is to hear.

Now half the day is night. Trees shed
their excess as leaves die in brilliance.

Notes

"Leaflet on Walking": The title riffs on the title of Lucie Brock-Broido's "Leaflet on Wooing."

"Our Grotto" is modeled on Pablo Neruda's "Te Recuerdo Como Eras," translated by W.S. Merwin as "I Remember You As You Were."

"Triple-Arch Bridge": Naturalist and author Frank Bolles (1856-1894) documented his walk to the Blue Hill (Milton, Massachusetts), crossing Paul's Bridge over the Neponset River, in *Land of the Lingering Snow* (1891).

"Please Explain": The piece of electronic music which so baffled my mother and me was John Cage's *Variations II*, as performed by David Tudor.

"The Small Hours of May": "The trees and I have woken up" comes from a poem by Cori Stenning Barnes.

"Ruined Piano" is inspired by *Night Kitchen*, a recording of music by Ross Bolleter (also a Zen Buddhist teacher in the Diamond Sangha lineage).

"Circa": Thanks to Elizabeth McKim for the idea of a sestina, the end words of which are solely prepositions.

"It's a Grand Night for Singing" is a song from the Rodgers and Hammerstein musical, *State Fair*.

Acknowledgments

Grateful acknowledgments are made to the publications in which these poems first appeared, many in earlier versions:

Autumn Sky Poetry Daily: "Another Poem About Fireflies," "Blue Fingertips," "Our Grotto"
Bagels with the Bards: "Almost Not Foreign," "You're It"
The Big Windows Review: "It's a Grand Night for Singing"
California Quarterly: "Half the Day is Night"
Constellations: "Look at the Sky"
Fox Chase Review: "Landscape With Hilton"
HedgeApple: "Third Story Roof Sitting"
Ibbetson Street: "Rest Stop, Tampa Bay," "Stony Brook, Granite," "Triple-Arch Bridge"
Lyrical Somerville: "Awake in the Sleeping Car"
Main Street Rag: "Girl and Grackle," "Ten at Night"
Meat for Tea: "An Eventual Introduction," "Friendly Ghosts," "Gaze, or Don't," "In Lieu of a Plane Crash," "Kneeling Woman and Dog," "None of My Business," "The Huffington Post or Whatever," "Translucent Man"

Naugatuck River Review: "Discarded School Instrument"

Nixes Mate Review: "Someone Else's Daughter," "Trailing Her Die"

riverbabble: "One Picture"

Redheaded Stepchild: "Leaflet on Walking"

Wilderness House Literary Review: "Absolutely No Idea," "Chance"

"Kneeling Woman and Dog" was also included in *Best Indie Lit New England*, volume 2.

"The Huffington Post or Whatever" is also included on Mass. Poetry's *Poem of the Moment* web site.

"Trailing Her Die" was also included in the *Nixes Mate Review Anthology 2017-18*.

"At Ten Degrees" and "See Your Hearing" were included in the chapbook, *The Afterimages* (Červená Barva Press, 2014).

My thanks go out to the many who have helped to shepherd these poems: Tom Daley and the members of the Tuesday evening workshop at the Boston Center for Adult Education; Zachary Bos and friends from the Boston Poetry Workshop; Kara Provost and my colleagues from the faculty creative writers' group at Curry College. The manuscript for this book benefited greatly from guidance and comments by April Ossman, Gary Duehr, Catherine Sasanov, and Barbara Helfgott Hyett. I'm grateful to Shana Hill for her support. First among all is my dear wife, Jane Wiley, who saw these poems before anyone else did, and steered many away from the pitiless rocks, or the doldrums, toward which they were headed.

About the Author

David P. Miller's chapbook *The Afterimages* was published by Červená Barva Press. He received degrees in theater at the University of Massachusetts/Amherst and Emerson College, and librarianship from Simmons College. For twenty-five years, he was a member of the Mobius Artists Group of Boston, creating his own performance art pieces and collaborating on performances of original experimental work, as well as pieces by John Cage, Gertrude Stein, and Jackson Mac Low. In 2018, he retired from Curry College in Milton, Massachusetts, where he was a librarian for twenty-six years. A resident of Boston since 1978, he lives in the Jamaica Plain neighborhood with his wife, the visual artist Jane Wiley.

42° 19' 47.9" N   70° 56' 43.9" W

Nixes Mate is a navigational hazard in Boston Harbor used during the colonial period to gibbet and hang pirates and mutineers.

Nixes Mate Books features small-batch artisanal literature, created by writers who use all 26 letters of the alphabet and then some, honing their craft the time-honored way: one line at a time.

nixesmate.pub/books

www.ingramcontent.com/pod-product-compliance
Lightning Source LLC
Chambersburg PA
CBHW050206130526
44591CB00035B/2330